Murder, Terror and Revenge in Medieval Lancashire

The Legend of Mab's Cross

by
Fred Holcroft

First published May 1992
by
Wigan Heritage Service
Dept. of Leisure
Wigan MBC
Trencherfield Mill
Wigan WN3 4EF

No part of this book may be reproduced, stored in a retrieval system, or transmitted in any form, or by any means, electronic, mechanical, photocopying, recording, or otherwise, without the prior permission of Wigan Heritage Service.

© Wigan Heritage Service, 1992.

ISBN 1 874496 00 5

Designed and produced by Coveropen Ltd., Wigan.
Tel: (0942) 821831

Contents

The Legend of Mab's Cross 5

The Chief Participants 8

The Banaster Rebellion 12

Bradshaw's Disappearance 20

The Return of William de Bradshaw 22

Coram Rege Roll 254 24

The End of the Story 29

To Moireen my wife

The Legend of Mab's Cross

Mab's Cross. From 'Traditions of Lancashire' (1829) by J.Roby.

AT the end of the film 'The Man Who Shot Liberty Valance' the editor of the local newspaper learns the truth about who really shot the old-time outlaw Liberty Valance. It was not, as everybody had been told, the timid storekeeper who went on to a great political career because of his brave deed, but a rancher who later died unknown and in poverty.

The newspaper editor is amazed. He stands up and says: "It makes no difference. When the truth is stranger than the legend — print the legend."

* * * *

The best known local legend, handed down from generation to generation, is the legend of Mab's Cross. How much of it is true and how much is just a story?

There are actually two versions of the Mab's Cross legend. The first is from the **Bradshaigh Roll,** a pedigree of the Bradshaw (or Bradshaigh) family made in 1647. It tells the story of Sir William

Sir William Bradshaghe 2d ✠ Mabell daughter and
Sone to Sr iohn was A   Sole heire of Hugh
great traueller and A   Noris de Haghe and
Souldyer and married   Blackrode and had issue
         To   JN. 8. E 2.

of this Mabel is a story by tradition of undouted
berity that in Sr William Bradshage's absence
(beinge 10 yeares away in the wares) she
married a welsh kt. Sr William retorninge
from the wares came in a Palmers habit amongst the Poore to haghe. Who when she saw &
congetringe that he faboured her former
husband wept, for which the kt chasticed her
at wich Sr William went and made him selfe
Knawne to his Tennants in woh space the kt
fled. but neare to Newton Parke Sr William ouer-
tooke him and slue him. The said Dame
Mabell was enioyned by her confessor to
doe Pennances by going onest euery week
barefout and bare legg'd to a Crosse ner Wigan
from the haghe wilest she liued & is called
Mabb I to this day; & ther monument Lyes
in wigan Church as you see ther Portrd

                                    An: Dom: 1315.

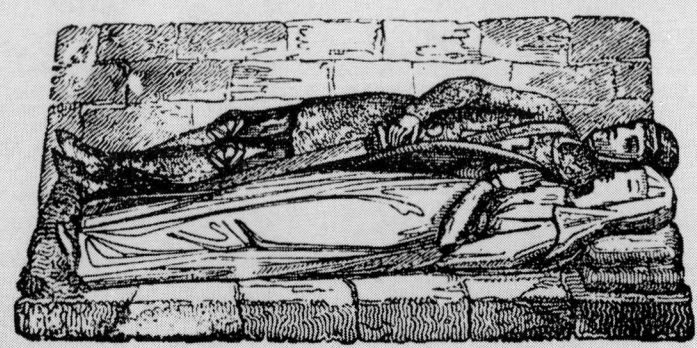

The text of the Bradshaigh Roll, and the Bradshaigh tomb, as they appeared in Sir Walter Scott's 'The Betrothed' (1825).

de Bradshaw who married Mabel, daughter of Hugh le Norreys of Haigh and Blackrod and who lived at Haigh Hall, near Wigan, during the reign of Edward II (1307-1327). A great soldier, Sir William went abroad to fight in 'the wares' and was reported killed. Lady Mabel took as her second husband a Welsh knight. Ten years later, Sir William returned to England and arrived at Haigh disguised as a palmer (a pilgrim carrying a palm-leaf in token of having been in the Holy Land). He was recognised by his tenants, whereupon the Welsh knight tried to escape. Sir William chased and caught up with him at Newton-le-Willows, where the Welshman was killed. Lady Mabel's confessor gave her the penance of walking once a week barefoot from Haigh Hall to a cross in Wigan which then became known as Mab's Cross.

In addition to this Bradshaigh version, handed down orally and written into the family tree in 1647, there is also the **Norris Declaration,** written by Sir William Norris of Speke in 1564. He had been told it some years earlier by his uncle Sir Roger Bradshaw. This version states that Sir William arrived at Haigh, and asked to see any woman named Norris (he having been promised the hand of Lady Mabel by the king); he was shown Mabel, who was busy baking oat-cakes in an oven. Sir William later went on a pilgrimage abroad for seven years; during his absence, Lady Mabel remarried. On his return Sir William proved his identity by showing his tenants a mark on his ribs. There was a fight at Newton-le-Willows where the Welsh knight was killed, after which Bradshaw rode to London to obtain the king's pardon. Oddly the Norris version does not mention Lady Mabel's penitent walk to the cross!

* * * *

Contemporary documents confirm that the two main characters mentioned in the legend were real persons and not invented ancestors or mythical figures. Sir William was the son of Sir Richard de Bradshaw of Westleigh and owned land in and around Haigh. Lady Mabel was the heiress of Hugh le Norreys, lord of the manor of Haigh and Blackrod.

History also confirms that these two real people were in fact separated for a long period of time — but not for the reason given in both versions of the story. The real reason was that in 1315 Sir William took part in a local revolt known as the Banaster Rebellion; not only was he declared an outlaw but his life was threatened by the enemies he had made.

The Chief Participants

AT the outset, let us look at the other chief participants in the story.

King Edward II

By the early 13th century the English barons had become so powerful that they were able to impose their will on King John and make him sign the Magna Carta in 1215. Two strong and powerful kings, Henry III (1216-1272) and his son Edward I (1272- 1307), won back control over the barons for the Crown; the next king, Edward II, however, was not made of such stern stuff.

Princes of the royal blood were named after the royal palace where they were born. Edward II was called Edward of Caernarvon. Born in 1284 he was the baby prince who was presented to the Welsh by his father Edward I:

> "I will give you a Prince,
> born in Wales who cannot
> speak a word of English"

(Unfortunately, this too is probably only a tale). No other English king has received such unanimous disapproval from contemporary chronicles and later writers. They all used phrases like "weak", "unfit to rule", "easily led". Yet he should have been a success. He was tall, muscular, good looking and intelligent. But he threw away all these advantages when he came to the throne.

English kings ruled through a 'household', a staff of advisers, and when his father died and he became king, Edward II brought into the royal court all his friends and acquaintances. Being lazy, only interested in fun and pleasure, Edward II left the running of the country to these men. This annoyed the barons, who regarded themselves as the natural advisers to the king. During Edward II's reign, they made many attempts to get rid of the king's favourites, or to make changes in the way that England was governed.

In 1312 they murdered his favourite Piers Gaveston. They claimed it was done because he was giving the king bad advice. Actually, Gaveston came from the province of Gascony, and although it was then ruled by the king of England, he was regarded as a 'foreigner'. They were also annoyed because he usually beat them at their hobby — jousting. Thomas, Earl of Lancaster, took a leading part in this, and Edward II never forgave him.

Thomas, Earl of Lancaster

Thomas, Earl of Lancaster was the most powerful nobleman in England, and the barons' natural leader. Because he was an important landowner in Lancashire, and his chief household official was a Lancashire knight, his activities are of great local interest. Thomas had many enemies in Lancashire, and his activities in the county against the Crown are a major factor in this story.

Thomas was no ordinary baron, as a glance at an extract from the royal family tree shows:

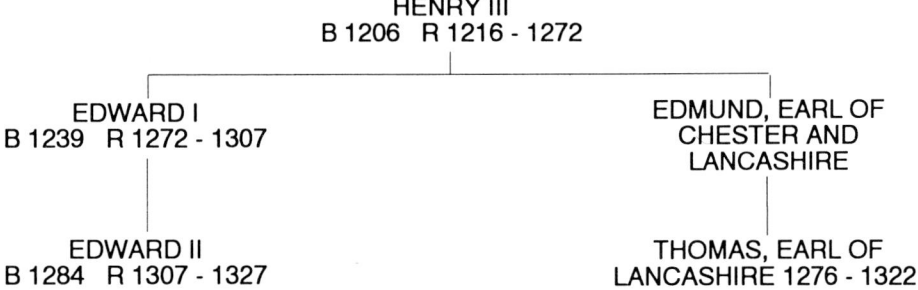

So Thomas, Earl of Lancaster was a grandson of one of England's greatest kings, Henry III, a nephew of another great king, Edward I, and a cousin of the new king, Edward II.

Thomas had five titles — he was Earl of Lancaster, Derby, Leicester, Lincoln and Salisbury. As such he was both extremely rich, with an income of over £11,000 a year, and powerful, with as many men in his private army as the king had in his permanent army! Born into great wealth, married to a rich heiress, a close relative of the king, Lancaster had everything going for him, yet he too did not fulfil his promise. He was unimaginative with little idea how to organise; cunning but not clever. He did not have a likeable character, being sulky, lazy, shifty, vicious, vindictive and disloyal.

Because the barons were in dispute with Edward II, it was inevitable that their natural leader, the Earl of Lancaster, would come into conflict with the king, and they soon grew to hate each other, especially after Gaveston's death in 1312.

Household Book of Thomas Earl of Lancaster.

	£	s.	d.		£	s.	d.
To charge of the pantry, buttery, and kitchen	3405	0	0	for the officers, and 4 ray cloths for carpets in the hall	345	13	8
184 tuns 1 pipe of red or claret wine, and 2 tuns of white wine	104	17	6	To 100 pieces of green silk for the knights, 14 budge furrs for surcoats, 13 hoods of budge furr for the clerks, 75 furrs of lamb for the livereys in summer, with canvas and cords to truss them	72	19	0
grocery, £180 17s. 0; six barrels of sturgeon, £19	199	17	0	saddles for the lord's summer livereys	51	6	8
6800 stockfishes, so called, and for dried fishes of all sorts, as lings, haberdenis, &c.	41	6	7	1 saddle for the earl of the prince's arms	2	0	0
1714 pounds of wax, vermilion & turpentine	314	7	4½	several items (the particulars in the account defaced)	241	14	1½
2319 pounds of tallow candles for the household, and 1870 of lights for Paris candles, called perchers	31	14	3	horses lost in ye service of the earl	8	6	8
charge of the earle's great horses, and servants' wages (generally 1500 horses)	486	4	3½	fees paid to earls, barons, knights, & esquires	623	15	5
linen for the earl and his chaplains	43	17	0	gifts to knights of France, the queen of England's nurses, to the countess of Warren, esquires, minstrels, messengers & riders	92	14	0
129 dozen of parchments and ink	4	8	3½	168 yards of russet cloth, and 24 coats for poor men, with money given the poor on Maundy Thursday	8	16	7
2 cloths of scarlet for the earl's use, 1 of russet for the bishop of Anjou, 70 of blue for the knights, 28 for the esquires, 15 of medley for the clerks, 15 for the officers, 19 for the grooms, 8 for the archers, 4 for the minstrels and carpenters, with the sharing and carridge for the earl's livery at Christmas	460	15	0	24 silver dishes, 24 saucers, 4 cups, 1 pair of pater nosters, 1 silver coffer; all bought this year	103	5	6
				divers messengers about the earl's business	34	19	8
				sundry things in the earl's chamber	5	0	0
7 furrs of variable miniver or powdered ermine, 7 hoods of purple, 395 furrs of budge for the livereys of barons, knights, and clerks, 123 furrs of lamb, bought at Christmas, for the esquires	147	17	8	several old debts paid this year	88	16	0¼
				the expenses of the countess at Pickering in the pantry, buttery, kitchen, &c.	285	13	4½
65 saffron-coloured cloths for the barons and knights in summer, 12 red cloths for the clerks, 26 ray cloths for the esquires, 1				wine, wax, spices, cloths, furrs, &c., for the countess's wardrobe	154	7	4½
					£7957	13	4½

Domestic expenses of the Earl of Lancaster for 1313. From 'Gregson's Portfolio of Fragments' (1869).

Sir Robert de Holland

Sir Robert de Holland was the head of a large and powerful Lancashire family, and he owned lands in Upholland, near Wigan, in Hale, near Liverpool and in Salmesbury, near Preston. Thomas, Earl of Lancaster, had made Sir Robert his chief household official, and gave him more lands in Lancashire, Cheshire and Staffordshire. He used his influence not only to obtain for Sir Robert various royal appointments, but also to arrange a marriage between Sir Robert and a very wealthy heiress who brought with her valuable properties in Oxfordshire, Northamptonshire and other counties all over England.

Soon, Holland's pride began to grow, and he began to use castles and lands in Lancashire which did not belong to him, but were the property of his master the Earl of Lancaster himself — the castle and borough of Liverpool, the manors of Everton, Crosby and Wavertree, the forest at Simonswood, the park of Toxteth and huge areas in Salford. He also interfered with the judicial process, granting pardons to criminals and ordering the deaths of his opponents.

This caused envy and jealousy among Holland's neighbours, and some began to be afraid of his power.

Sir Adam Banaster

Sir Adam Banaster was a local landowner, with property in Shevington, Heath Charnock, Adlington and Duxbury, near Wigan. Although Sir Adam was married to Holland's sister, which made him Sir Robert's brother-in-law, there were many disputes between the Hollands and the Banasters, and their family feud was to become the focus of one of the most savage episodes in the history of Lancashire — a story of **murder, terror and revenge**.

The coat-of-arms of the Bradshaws during the Middle Ages consisted of two black diagonal lines and three black birds on a white background.

The Banaster Rebellion

BY the year 1315, England, and especially Lancashire, was in a state of turmoil. Edward II's English army had been defeated at the Battle of Bannockburn in the previous year, so that not only was Scotland now an independent country, but Scottish armies raided into Northern England, and Robert the Bruce's brother was invited by the Irish to be their king and throw the English out. English national prestige had sunk to a new low.

The Earl of Lancaster was determined to make the king dismiss his unpopular advisers and give power back to the barons. Private feuds broke out between those who supported the king and those who wanted change. Besides these political troubles, economic and social distress caused by exceptional climatic conditions brought widespread ruin to the people. Heavy rain and floods destroyed crops, sheep and cattle died of plague, food became scarce, death from starvation and disease affected all classes. The Government was helpless to deal with the situation.

All over England the king's castles were attacked by his enemies, and he was unable to uphold law and order in many parts of the country. In Lancashire, a revolt broke out, not against the king but against his chief opponent Thomas, Earl of Lancaster, and in particular the Earl's chief household official, Sir Robert de Holland.

The motives for the rising are not very clear — the leaders said that they were acting on behalf of the king but it is probable that they were jealous of the Earl of Lancaster's top man, Holland, who had been given so many favours over them. The rebel's leader, Sir Adam Banaster, was also hoping to avoid prosecution for murder. Banaster's two chief lieutenants were Sir Henry de Lea of Charnock Richard and Sir William Bradshaw of Haigh and Blackrod, husband of Lady Mabel. These three met with others at Westhoughton on 8 October 1315 and swore an oath of loyalty to one another. Then began one month of anarchy in Lancashire, with the complete breakdown of law and order.

On 12 October, four days after their first meeting, they sent a party of soldiers under the command of Nicholas de Singleton and John de Croston to Radcliffe, near Manchester. Their mission was to kidnap Adam de Radcliffe and his brothers, but events did not go to plan. They captured Adam but when they searched the house of Sir Henry de Bury for the brothers, they could not find them, and in a fight which followed, Henry de Bury was killed and his horse and other possessions stolen.

Law and order had not yet completely broken down in Lancashire — four men were tried and hanged for the crime: John de Croston, Stephen Scallard, William Tegge and Richard Asshes. Sir William de Bradshaw was declared an outlaw because he did not turn up in court to face accusations against him.

The book 'Vita Edwardi Secundi', written c.1325 by a monk living at Malmesbury, states:

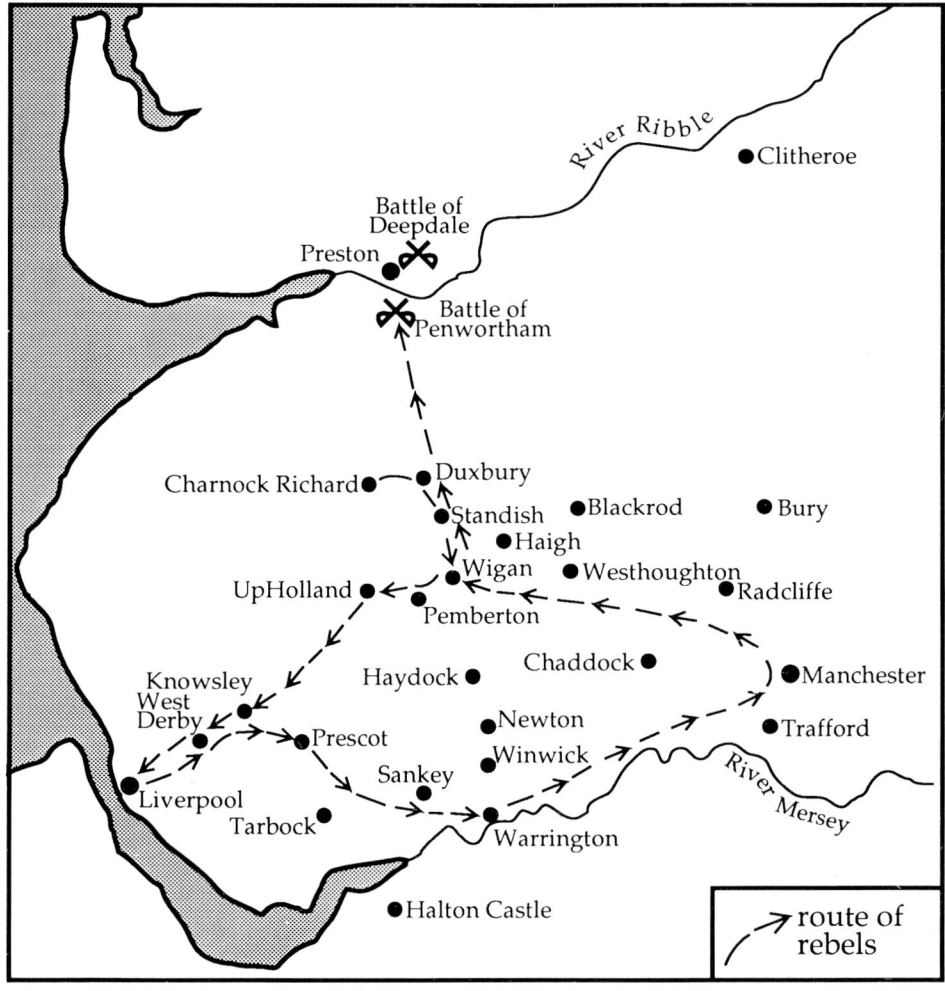

Map showing the route taken by the rebel forces.

"It happened meanwhile that a certain knight Adam Banaster by name, of the household retinue of the Earl of Lancaster committed homicide. Despairing of pardon he rose against his lord for he believed that it would please the king if he showed himself hostile to the earl who had so often opposed the king and forced him to alter plans already set on foot.Some eight hundred men were persuaded to help him, some bought by bribes, some compelled by fear of death, who had either to leave the country or join him in arms."

So it looks as if the incident which caused Bradshaw to be outlawed was the attempt by the rebels, including Bradshaw himself, to coerce others to join them.

Ten days later, on 22 October 1315, the rebels met once more at the home of Adam Banaster and next day they set off to terrorize the followers of Thomas, Earl of Lancaster, especially Sir Robert de Holland and his close associates. Joined by four knights from the Bickerstaffe family, they rode to Wigan where they stole eight oxen, four cows, corn and goods together worth £60 from John del Crosse (who probably lived in Standishgate) and robbed the house of Thurston de Northlegh (Norley) at Pemberton (lo-

Clitheroe Castle was captured by the rebel forces on 26 October 1315. From 'Gregson's Portfolio of Fragments' (1869).

Liverpool Castle successfully resisted an attack by the rebels. From 'Gregsons Portflio of Fragments' (1869).

cated at the junction of City Road and Norley Road, near the present site of Pemberton Community High School), taking 16 oxen, 12 cows and other goods together worth £40.

The rebels then divided their forces. One party of knights with their mounted followers captured Clitheroe Castle, owned by the Earl of Lancaster — at that time one of the strongest castles in Lancashire — and carried off the weapons and equipment stored there. A second party moved south-west from Wigan towards Liverpool, plundering the countryside as they went to keep their army supplied. The two parties rejoined one another and Adam de Banaster led them in an attack on Liverpool Castle but they were beaten off. They obtained £10 each from West Derby and Knowsley in return for not destroying the settlements.

Moving towards Warrington, the leaders showed the people a letter with the royal seal at the bottom, which they claimed gave the rebels the king's permission for what they were doing. This did not prevent them from stealing oxen, cattle, and goods worth 100 marks from Ellen de Tarbock and others. For four days the rebel army remained at Warrington, in control of the only bridge across the River Mersey, sending out raiding parties in all directions to plunder and terrorize the countryside, especially the supporters of the Earl of Lancaster and Sir Robert de Holland, but also any unfortunate neutrals who got in their way.

One day a party led by Thomas Banaster and Henry de Lea captured Halton Castle — owned by the Earl of Lancaster — by setting fire to the gates, and carried off the military supplies which were stored there. Another party led by William de Bradshaw raided Haydock and Newton-le-Willows, stealing oxen, cattle, sheep, corn and other goods from the manor of Sir William de Holland (Sir Robert's brother) and from Sir John de Langton. A third party stole supplies from the barns at Sankey, near Warrington, owned by Sir Thomas de Hale.

The ruins of Halton Castle, near Runcorn, which the rebels succeeded in capturing on 27 October 1315 by setting fire to the gates. From Thomas Baines's 'Lancashire and Cheshire Past and Present' (1868-9).

For three more days they continued to behave like this, stealing, extorting money and threatening the local inhabitants. Then on 31 October 1315 the rebel army moved on towards Manchester, plundering as it went, especially the lands of Sir Henry de Trafford who lived in Stretford (near the present site of Manchester United's ground). At Manchester the rebels showed a banner painted with the king's coat of arms, which they said the king had sent them, in another attempt to convince people that they were acting on his behalf.

The Earl of Lancaster's supporters now recovered from the shock of the attacks on them and began to retaliate. While the rebels were at Manchester, Thurston de Norley led an armed band into Wigan and robbed a number of the townspeople, while Robert de Holland made straight for William de Bradshaw's lands in Haigh and Blackrod and stole from there. The Earl himself collected his trusted followers into an army. The most important official in the county, Edmund Nevill, sheriff of Lancaster, was supposed to enforce law and order, but he was having difficulty getting his army together. The sheriff sent a force led by three knights, Sir Adam de Huddleston, Sir Walter de Vavasour and Sir Richard le Waleys against the rebel army.

The rebels got to hear of this and hurriedly left Manchester, pausing on the way to rob Wigan once more, Gilbert de Culcheth being the unlucky victim on this occasion. They attacked Huddleston's small force at Penwortham, near Preston, and completely defeated it. Huddleston and Waleys were captured, Ralph de Milton and Adam Wynkidlee were killed; Vavasour died later of his wounds, and the rest of the army ran away. This was when another knight, Richard de Bolton, drowned as he tried to swim his horse across the River Ribble. The rebels also captured horses, weapons and other items of equipment left on the battlefield by the defeated army. Entering Preston in high spirits they continued their policy of robbing and obtaining money by threats.

The sheriff had now raised a small army, a 'posse comitatus' of 300 men, which contained some good soldiers led by Sir William Dacre, Sir John and Sir Michael Harrington. The two sides met at Deepdale, just outside Preston, on 5 November 1315 and in less than an hour the rebels were defeated. Several of the leaders, including Nicholas de Singleton and Ralph de Bickerstaffe were killed, Thomas Banaster was taken prisoner, but the three original ringleaders all escaped. Sir William de Bradshaw did not hesitate. Already declared an outlaw for his part in the murder of Henry de Bury, and therefore liable to be killed on sight, he did not stop running until he had left England. He was not to return for seven years.

The other two ringleaders, Adam Banaster and Henry de Lea, were not so lucky. They hid out in the woods for a week before taking refuge in the house of Henry de Euferlong in Charnock Richard. Henry betrayed them to the searchers, who took them to Layland Moor where they were both executed. Their sworn enemy, the formidable Thurston de Norley, took the dead men's clothing, jewellery, daggers and weapons.

In the aftermath of the rebellion, Lancaster's supporters now began to take terrible retribution from their beaten opponents. Robert de Holland had not taken part in the Battle of Deepdale, but he now organised the pursuit, leading 2,000 armed men who roamed the countryside in search of fugitives from the battle. He used the opportunity to take revenge not only on his opponents, but also on those who were suspected of being so, and even on those who had stayed out of the conflict altogether. Unstoppable, they stole horses, oxen, cattle, gold, silver, cloth and other goods totalling in value over £5,000 — an enormous sum of money in those days, when a ploughman's annual wage was five shillings.

One of the first former rebels to suffer was Henry Nightingale of Hoscar, who was captured and executed on the spot without trial. Two other ex-rebels, Roger de Lever and Henry de Urmston, were also beheaded immediately on capture. Is it any wonder that Sir William de Bradshaw took to his heels with all this going on?

With three ringleaders dead, a fourth in prison, a fifth exiled abroad and their followers killed or helpless, the revolt had been well and truly crushed — the Holland faction was on top again. For the next six years his supporters behaved more or less as they liked, and the more violent elements committed all kinds of crimes in the secure knowledge that they were not likely to be punished. One of their crimes was extortion, whereby they entered workshops demanding the goods at less than the proper price. Another practice was to obtain money with menaces — to beat or to threaten to beat people if they did not give money. This extortion of money raised huge sums from their richer enemies. They attacked farmers working peacefully in their fields and even robbed the refugees who were streaming through Lancashire after abandoning their homes in the border counties because of Scottish raids.

Holland's supporters were able to get themselves into positions of authority in the county and used these positions to obtain money illegally. When officially authorized to obtain supplies for the king's army fighting the Scots, they embezzled the money. When enlisting men to fight in the army, they took bribes from some and allowed them to avoid military service. When appointed as tax-collectors, they kept some of the money for themselves and took bribes from taxpayers, allowing them to pay less than they ought. When they should have been arresting real criminals, they let them go after taking bribes from them, and threatened to arrest innocent travellers if they did not pay up. They also abused their official position in other ways. One of the duties of the sheriff of Lancashire was to travel round the county with a small force to make sure that all was well, and he was given free board and lodgings in each village for up to three nights. When William le Gentil became sheriff he stayed for over a week with a force twice as large as was needed, living extravagantly and causing unnecessary expense.

The behaviour of Thomas de Hale as coroner was even worse. Instead of examining a corpse found dead by accident or murder, as was his duty, he sent a servant, who ordered it to be buried. He often refused to give a verdict until he had been paid 12d. In those days the coroner was very important because his decision on the cause of death could influence the inheritance of huge amounts.

When they had nothing else to do, the supporters of Robert de Holland fought amongst themselves. On one occasion, for example, Adam de Hindley and Hugh de Tyldesley fought a battle at Chaddock Hurst, near Atherton, with casualties on both sides. Their favourite illegal pastime was poaching. The court records are filled with references to stealing game and venison either from their enemies' parks or from the forests reserved for the king. Thurston de Norley's reeve was attacked trying to defend his master's deer park in Pemberton and brought to court for poaching from the king's deer park in Upholland shortly afterwards. When the courts tried to act they intimidated the jurors. Armed gangs arrived at the Assizes and the jurors were too frightened to reach a 'guilty' verdict. Sometimes a simple bribe to the jurors worked instead. They even cheated at the parliamentary elections. Two of the faction were nominated to represent Lancashire without a proper election being held, and they even claimed expenses to which they were not entitled!

Bradshaw's Disappearance

WHERE did Bradshaw go? There is no documentary evidence of his presence in Lancashire between 1315 and 1322 — about seven years, the same length of time as mentioned in the 'Norris Declaration'. Both versions tell how Bradshaw went on the Crusades, "to the Holy Wars" (Bradshaigh version) or "to the Holy Places" (Norris version). The Crusades to Palestine, however, were long since over.

There were other wars which were given the title 'crusades' — in southern Spain against the Moors, in Prussia and Poland against the pagan Slavs — and he could have gone to one of these places. At the time of Bradshaw's disappearance there was a campaign in Wales to put down the rebellion of Llewellyn Bryn against the English. In those days military service (usually unpaid) for the Crown was a condition of obtaining a royal pardon. Or perhaps Bradshaw hired himself as a mercenary to a foreign country — a common practice in the Middle Ages.

In 1318, about three years after his disappearance, Bradshaw was pardoned by Edward II. Yet he did not return; his enemies ignored the pardon and stole his land. Nevertheless, the 'Norris version' mentions a pardon, even though it was for something else.

Did people believe that Bradshaw had died? This was given as the reason for Lady Mabel's re-marriage. In 1319, four years after his disappearance, in a lawsuit about the manor of Anderton, there are two references to Sir William as if he were dead:

> 1) "except William de Bradshaigh who is dead".
> 2) "the said William de Bradshaigh was holding the same land with Mabel, which William is now dead".

Lady Mabel appeared in court over this lawsuit, and so it would seem that she, and everyone else concerned, thought that William de Bradshaw was dead by the year 1319, even though he had been pardoned a year earlier. Or was she just pretending to protect him from his enemies?

Did Lady Mabel remarry? Both versions of the legend say that Lady Mabel married for the second time after wrongly assuming that her first husband William de Bradshaw was dead. No historical document has been found to support a second marriage.

Two possibilities put forward by historians as to who might have been the second husband — Sir Peter Lymesey and Sir Edmund Nevill — were both married to wives who were alive during the entire period. Moreover, neither could have been killed by Bradshaw immediately on his return in 1322, as Lymesey lived until 1324 and Nevill until 1336 (he outlived Bradshaw).

Times were difficult for an unprotected woman during the Middle Ages, especially if she owned property or land. Perhaps, although she did not remarry, Lady Mabel lived with another knight who protected her against her husband's enemies?

Some of William de Bradshaw's lands were confiscated by his enemies and given to other knights. At first Lady Mabel was allowed to live on them, then later she was thrown off! Bradshaw's lands at Haigh and Blackrod were given to Peter de Lymesey and because Lady Mabel was still in residence the clerk in a court case of 1318 wrote down by mistake "Peter de Lymesey and Mabel his wife". In a second court case a month later, however, she is referred to as "Mabel de Haigh". As for Sir Edmund Nevill, he did in fact marry Euphemia, widow of Orm de Kellet who had died in prison.

When did Lady Mabel end her days? In 1348 she is recorded as paying the usual 10 pence fee due from the manor of Haigh. 1349 was the year of the Black Death, and her name is not mentioned in records again.

Did Lady Mabel do penance at Mab's Cross? A Wigan deed dated 6 April 1403 mentions "two acres of land near Mabcrosse worth 4s". As Lady Mabel had probably died in 1349, the cross would therefore have been known as Mab's Cross within the lifetime of at least some people who had personally known her. It seems highly unlikely, then, that the name is an invention.

There is evidence that a cross existed at Wigan before Lady Mabel's time. There is a reference of 1277 to Adam del Cross, who owned a plot of land "opposite the Cross between the highway and the River Douglas".

Also, as the figure of a woman kneeling in front of a stone cross was carved on the side of the Bradshaigh tomb in Wigan Parish Church, it does indeed seem likely that Lady Mabel did penance there.

In her later years Lady Mabel became known for her charitable acts. She built chapels at Blackrod and Wigan. Were these also acts of penance?

The Return of William De Bradshaw

IN 1322, seven years after the Banaster Rebellion, the Earl of Lancaster decided to overthrow Edward II but completely mismanaged the whole conspiracy. Lancaster's army was beaten at the Battle of Boroughbridge, outside York. (This little-known battle was the first occasion that knights fought on foot alongside their infantry, using the tactics which were later to bring famous victories at Crecy and Agincourt). The night before the battle many of Lancaster's men deserted to the other side; among the first to go over was Sir Robert de Holland. Holland's treachery did not do him any good — Edward put him in prison anyway. Lancaster was captured and later executed.

With one enemy dead and another in prison Sir William de Bradshaw returned. Although Bradshaw had been pardoned in 1318 he had not dared to return, a wise decision considering what had happened to Sir Alexander de Turton who had hidden for a year after the rebellion had been put down, only to be murdered by Holland's supporters on his return to Lancashire.

With the return of Sir William de Bradshaw open warfare broke out once more in Lancashire. Bradshaw went immediately to his old estate at Blackrod and got together his old comrades, the Anderton family, the Banasters, the Bickerstaffes, the Mawdesleys and the Worthingtons. The Hollands met up again with the Tyldesleys and the Hindleys, and of course with the irrepressible Thurston de Norley. As Robert de Holland was in prison his brother took command.

In January 1323 the two sides fought near Warrington; Holland's squire was wounded and Bradshaw captured two of Holland's horses. In retaliation Holland attacked Bradshaw's manor house at Blackrod but was beaten off, losing two men. Some months later they again attacked Bradshaw at Leyland Church, killing one of his men and stealing his horse. The fighting continued throughout the year. The Hollands repeatedly attacked Bradshaw's supply trains, stealing his goods. Bradshaw retaliated by poaching deer from Thurston de Norley, murdering his supporters when he caught them off guard, robbing others and holding some to ransom in his fortified manor house at Blackrod. As if this private feud was not bad enough for the ordinary people, both Bradshaw and Holland victimized them as the latter had done earlier, and threatened the courts in order to escape justice.

In October 1323, encouraged to stamp on the lawlessness and chaos by his easy victory over the Earl of Lancaster, the king himself managed to partially defuse the situation. In those days the king's court (coram rege) could be held all over the country — wherever, in fact, the king was present. Edward II decided to visit Lancashire himself and to hold his investigations at the town which had been the centre of the recent disturbances — Wigan.

The king sent several trusted servants to take statements from the people and write down their complaints. The two most important officials were Sir Henry de Scrope, elder brother of the king's chief judge and Robert de Ayleston, the king's clerk, who had done similar work in other parts of the country. They called together a panel of 48 knights who made up several juries to hear these complaints.

On 22 October 1323, almost eight years to the day since the outbreak of the Banaster Rebellion, the king's court met in Wigan. The presence of the king himself and his personal guards — heavily armed, highly trained fighting men — was intended to overawe the two sides. Edward II stayed at Upholland, in the manor house of the imprisoned Robert de Holland. He would only have attended in person for the first few days when the major crimes were dealt with, then left; the rest of the cases were heard by Scrope and Ayleston.

None of the survivors, either from the Banaster Rebellion of 1315 or the civil war which had raged in Lancashire between 1315 and 1323, was severely punished. Poaching seems to have attracted the most attention. There are more accusations of, and covictions for, poaching than for any other type of offence. Sentences passed on convicted poachers were more severe than for many other categories of offence. Thurston de Norley was only fined for embezzling £100 while he was collecting taxes for the king, but was sent to prison for an indefinite time (at the king's pleasure) for poaching three stags from Myerscough Park, the king's private hunting forest.

Coram Rege Roll 254

The court proceedings were written in detail on 34 parchment sheets (membranes) which survive to this day at the Public Record Office in London. The 'filing system' used was made by making a hole in the top corner and threading the sheets together with parchment string. Each sheet is just over 8" (22 cms) wide but they vary in length, the shortest being 18" (45 cms) long, while most are between 23" and 30" (60 cms and 75 cms).

The sheets were originally numbered 1 to 34 in 14th century handwriting; in the 17th century they were re-numbered 40 to 74. In the second numbering, however, 10 is not re-numbered, while 42 and 49 are not used. All the sheets have writing on both sides except 4, 22, 23 and 27. Handwriting is in the neat, clear style of the 14th century scribes, but is not by the same person. Several clerks were used to make a fair copy from the rough notes made in court, and often blank spaces were left for later additions. There are many corrections and short notes in the margin.

The sheets are not arranged in chronological order, and few have dates, so it is difficult to tell the order of the court proceedings. Mostly, the sheets have headings to show the different groups and type of offenders proceeded against, and the hundred or township from which the jurors came.

The roll begins with the Articles of Inquiry and the King's Writ, which had to be written down to show the reason for the court being held and to prove that it was official and genuine.

Written in a quaint mixture of Latin and French, these set out all the types of crimes which were to be investigated. (see overleaf)

* * * *

Many offenders escaped unpunished. If the court's success is measured by the number of defendants found guilty then it was most certainly unsuccessful. Why?

- Many defendants refused to appear and the sheriff was ordered to find them and bring them in. Such entries are marked:

    "capiantur" *(they are to be arrested)*
    "exigantur" *(they are told to appear)*
    "inquiratur" *(an inquiry is to be made)*

- Many cases never came to trial but were put off until later.

These entries are marked:

> **"alibi plenius"** *(dealt with more fully in another place)*

- Many defendants claimed that they had already been pardoned by the king for the offences for which they had been brought before the court! Royal pardons were sometimes granted to those who had fought on the king's side, either during the recent disturbances or in the campaigns against the Scottish and Welsh. Such entries are marked:

> **"pdon"** or **"perdonatus"** *(pardoned)*

- Many of the accused claimed 'privilege of clergy', that as clerks in holy orders they came under the jurisdiction of the church courts and not the king's court (coram rege) which therefore had no right to try or punish them. Many produced written proof of their status from their parish priest or even from their bishop. As a result, many defendants were either not tried or found not guilty, while others were convicted but handed over to the church court to be sentenced. These entries are marked:

> **"fuit clericus"** *(clerk)*
> **"lra epi"** or **"littra episcopi"** *(bishop's letter)*
> **"clic con"** or **"clericus convictus"** *(convicted clerk)*

- The vast majority of cases were found 'not guilty' or 'acquitted' by the juries and the defendants were set free. There were many reasons for this, particularly:

  — the long length of time that had passed since many offences had taken place (one was stated to have been in 1290) meant that the evidence against the accused would have been flimsy.

  — a degree of corruption and intimidation in the judicial system which even the king's personal officials and soldiers could not stop.

  Some defendants were able to give good reasons why they should be acquitted. For instance, one man got off by proving that his victim had been previously outlawed and never pardoned (it was not a crime to kill anyone declared an outlaw). For all those who were found 'not guilty' the entries are marked:

> **"Q"** or **"quietus"** *(acquitted)*

- Even in the cases of those who were found 'guilty' many were let off with fines and not imprisoned or executed even though their crimes carried the death sentence. This was particularly the case when dealing with the richer, more prominent wrongdoers. Naturally the fines in some instances were huge, but many fines were so small as to be laughable. They can only have been token punishments. It was intended that those convicted

continued on page 28

ARTICLES OF INQUIRY

Dominus Rex misit iusticiariis suis hic apud Wygan nunciante magistro Roberto de Ayleson' custode privati sigilli sui quosdam articulos inquirendos in forma que subsequitur:
(1) Des homicides roberies et totes maneres de felonies par queux faites de quei et ou et de queu temps.
(2) Item de ceux que prenent et prendre fount a les oeps le Roy ou a lour enfauncz ou a nul autre ou a lour oeps demeigne les biens dautri conntre lour gree saunz paiement ou gree faire et la manere de la prise.
(3) Item de cequx qe prenent et ount pris de gentz pour faire desport des prises susditez et fount prises des poures.
(4) Item de ceux qe prenent certeyn des villes pur eux desporter de tieles prises et vount as autres villes qe meyns ou riens ne les volent doner.
(5) Item de ceux qe ount poer deslire gentz daler en la guerre le Roy et ount riens pris de suffrer en oster les vns et prendre les autres.

The Lord King sent to his justices here at Wigan by word of Master Robert de Ayleston, keeper of his privy seal, certain articles of inquiry in the form which follows:
(1) Concerning homicides, robberies and all manner of felonies, by whom, of what nature, where and at what time committed.
(2) Likewise concerning such as take or cause to be taken to the use of the king, or of their children or of any other, or to their own use, the goods of others against their will without making payment or satisfaction therefore, and the manner of the prise.
(3) Likewise concerning such as take or having taken [anything] from people in order to grant exemption from the prises abovesaid and take prises from the poor.
(4) Likewise concerning such as take from certain towns in order to exempt them for such prises and go to other towns which will give them less or nothing [to be exempted].
(5) Likewise concerning such as have power to choose men to go to the king's wars and have taken anything to allow some to withdraw [themselves] therefrom and to take others.

WRIT ON BEHALF OF THE KING

Dominus Rex mandauit breue suum Justiciariis suis hic in hec verba: Edwardus dei gratia rex Anglie dominus Hibernie et dux Aquitanie justiciariis suis ad placita coram nobis tenenda assignatis, salutem. Cum occasione turbacionis in regno nostro nuper mote contra nos per quosdam inimicos et rebelles nostros ac nobis contrariantes felonie, roberie ac alia mala et transgressiones diverse nobis et populo nostro in diversis partibus regni nostri extiterint perpetrate in nostri dampnum et populi predicti oppressionem et contra pacem nostram; Nos super huiusmodi malis remedium quod poterimus apponere volentes et ea puniri prout decet vobis mandamus firmiter iniungentes quod in comitatibus Lanc', Derb' et Staff' et alibi in regno nostro quociens vos infra idem regnum transire contigerit ad placita huiusmodi tenenda de feloniis, roberiis et transgressionibus predictis, ac prisis, conspiratoribus, conuenticulis et confederacionibus exnunc per singula loca per que transieritis tam infra libertates quam extra cum omni diligencia et modis quibus poteritis inquiratis iuxta articulos vobis inde liberatos, et querelas omnium et singulorum in hac parte se conqueri volencium audiatis et iusticiam et racionem faciatis et omnes illos quos inde coram vobis conuinci contigerit tam ad sectam nostram quam aliorum puniatis secundum legem et consuetudinem regni nostri, sessiones vestras de loco in locum et de die in diem quousque premissa finaliter terminentur modo debito tam extra dies termini consueti quam infra facientes. Teste me ipso apud Skipton' in Crauen' primo die Octobris anno regni nostir decimo septimo.

The Lord King sent his writ to his justices here in these words: Edward, by the grace of God king of England, lord of Ireland and duke of Aquitaine, to his justices appointed to hold the pleas before us, greeting. Whereas by reason of the disturbance lately fomented against us in our realm by certain persons our enemies, rebels, and contrarians, felonies, robberies and other evils and divers trespasses have been committed against us and our people in sundry parts of our realm to our loss and the oppression of the aforesaid people and against our peace; We, willing to apply what remedy we can to such evils and to inflict appropriate punishment therefor, command you firmly enjoining that, as often as you may happen to journey within the same realm in the counties of Lancaster, Derby and Stafford and elsewhere in our realm to hold such pleas, you shall immediately in the several places through which you journey, both within the liberties and without, inquire with all diligence and by whatever means you can concerning the aforesaid felonies, robberies and trespasses and concerning prises, conspirators, assemblies and confederacies according to the articles thereon delivered unto you, and shall hear the plaints of all and singular persons who wish to complain in this matter, and shall do justice and reason and punish all those who may be convicted thereof before you at our suit and at the suit of others according to the law and custom of our realm, holding your sessions from place to place and from day to day, as well after as during the days of the customary term, until the premises be finally determined in due form. Witness myself at Skipton in Craven, the first day of October in the seventeenth year of our reign.

should definitely pay the fine. Every time a fine was imposed the amount was stated on the roll together with the names of those who were to stand surety if the defendant did not pay. These entries are marked:

    "fin" or "finis" *(fine)*

- There is vivid proof of the unfairness of the court proceedings. It can be clearly seen from reading this document that the rich and powerful on the whole escaped punishment, while the poor and those without influence received the heaviest sentences. No rich men were executed. Every instance of execution shows that the convicted person was poor — even penniless. Such entries are marked:

    "catalla nulla" *(no chattels)*
    "S^s" or "suspensus" *(hanged)*
    "suspendatur" *(he is to be hanged)*

- A few of the accused never came to trial because it was proved that they were dead. In these cases the entries are marked:

    "obierunt" *(they are dead)*

- One last attempt to bring the accused to justice was to have them declared 'outlaws', that is 'outside the law'; anyone could then kill them on sight without fear of punishment. Outlaws, therefore, either had to surrender quickly to stop people going after them, or go into hiding. A public announcement was made in four successive county courts, asking them to "come before the king's peace" and if they failed to appear, they were outlawed. Such entries are marked:

    "exigantur" "exigant" "ex. gan." "ex. g." *(told to appear)*

The End of the Story

ALTHOUGH the court failed to bring justice to the down-trodden inhabitants of 14th century Lancashire, the records of proceedings are invaluable as almost the only source of information now available recording the events in Lancashire between 1315 and 1323.

The end of the story is found in other documents but it is worth describing. It concerns the last two characters to disappear from the scene — Robert de Holland and William de Bradshaw. Holland had been imprisoned for his part in the revolt against Edward II, even though he had changed sides at the last minute. He was released in 1328 and spent most of his time on his estates in the south of England. This may have been part of the terms of his release (he had to reside where the king could keep an eye on him) or perhaps he could have decided it was safer to stay away from Lancashire. In any case, it did him no good. Bradshaw and his allies were not the only ones who hated Holland. His former friends had never forgiven Sir Robert for deserting Thomas, Earl of Lancaster on the night before the battle, and it was they who ambushed and killed him at Henley-on-Thames in 1328.

The Bloody Stone, Newton-le-Willows. It was here that, according to legend, Sir William Bradshaw killed the Welsh knight who had bigamously married Lady Mabel.

William de Bradshaw suffered a similar fate. Ten years after the court proceedings against him had failed, he was still quarrelling and fighting with his neighbours, but in 1333 he fought his last battle near Newton-le-Willows, the scene of so many of his earlier exploits. He was ambushed and killed by a large band of horsemen — over 40 are named in the court records — as yet another old score was settled. The attackers were all either relatives or friends of the late Sir Henry de Bury who had been killed almost 20 years earlier! Lives were short but memories were long in the Middle Ages.

For hundreds of years a large red boulder on the pavement by the side of the main Winwick-Newton road at Newton-le-Willows, known locally as the 'bloody stone', was supposedly stained by the dead knight's blood. Both versions of the Mab's Cross legend tell how Lady Mabel's second husband was killed at Newton-le-Willows — how ironic that it was Bradshaw himself who was killed there!

* * * *

For centuries the bodies of Sir William and Lady Mabel lay side by side in Wigan Parish Church. Their tomb was situated in the Bradshaigh Chapel. This was originally a chantry or chapel specially set apart for mass to be said for the relief of souls in purgatory. It was founded by Lady Mabel for the benefit of the soul of her late husband. On their tomb was a panel which tradition says represents the slaying of the Welsh knight by Sir William. In reality the scene probably depicted Sir William's own death.

The Bradshaigh Monument in Wigan Parish Church c.1950. The carved panels on the sides of the tomb can be clearly seen.

* * * *

Mab's Cross in its previous position, before it was moved to facilitate road improvements in 1921.

What of Mab's Cross itself?. For hundreds of years it has stood by the main north road out of Wigan, exposed to the elements and vandalism. In 1921 it was moved for safekeeping inside the railings of Wigan Girls' High School (now Mab's Cross Primary School), on the opposite side of the road.

It remains today, as a constant reminder of times past. Does it bring to mind the romantic legend of the childhood sweethearts, separated, only to be reunited? Or the story of murder, terror and revenge in medieval Lancashire?

WIGAN HERITAGE SERVICE

The Metropolitan Wigan area has a long and rich history, and interest in our local heritage has never been higher. Wigan Heritage Service, comprising the Archives, Museums and Local History services, seeks to preserve this heritage and to interpret it to as wide an audience as possible. The Heritage Service has major public outlets in Wigan and Leigh.

THE HISTORY SHOP

This new heritage development is located in the Old Library, Rodney Street, Wigan — a splendid Alfred Waterhouse building of 1878. The History Shop is, we believe, the first of its kind in Britain. It offers the following attractions:

- a state of the art display, telling the story of the Wigan area from the earliest times to the present day
- a temporary display area, in which the Service's art collection figures prominently
- a study/research centre, incorporating the Wigan Local History collection and a genealogical centre of excellence
- a small retail outlet, selling a range of heritage-related merchandise, including books, photographs and quality souvenirs
- a meeting/lecture room, with a programme of public lectures and displays; this room is also available for hire by local societies and groups.

The History Shop has something for everyone — young or old, local or non-local. For further information, please telephone **(0942) 828128**.

THE ARCHIVES AND LOCAL HISTORY SERVICE, LEIGH

Original archival documents for the Metropolitan Wigan area can be consulted in the Archives Service searchroom in Leigh Town Hall. These include records of churches, schools, societies and businesses, official council archives, papers of local families, estates and individuals and copies of census returns. For further information, please telephone **(0942) 672421 ext 266.**

Leigh Local History Service operates from the Turnpike Centre, Leigh Library. The collection includes local books and pamphlets, maps, photographs, newspapers and copies of parish registers and census returns. To find out more, telephone **(0942) 604131**.

Other Heritage Service attractions include Astley Green Colliery, Hindley Museum and The Stables Centre, Haigh Country Park. For further details of these, telephone **(0942) 828128**.

REMEMBER — *You* can be of service to the Heritage Service. If you have any items in which you think we might be interested, please do not hesitate to contact us, on **(0942) 828128.**